W9-AHE-147

ANIMALS OF THE DESERT
Roadrunners
by Patrick Perish
BLASTOFF! READERS
2
BELLWETHER MEDIA • MINNEAPOLIS, MN

Note to Librarians, Teachers, and Parents:

Blastoff! Readers are carefully developed by literacy experts and combine standards-based content with developmentally appropriate text.

Level 1 provides the most support through repetition of high-frequency words, light text, predictable sentence patterns, and strong visual support.

Level 2 offers early readers a bit more challenge through varied simple sentences, increased text load, and less repetition of high-frequency words.

Level 3 advances early-fluent readers toward fluency through increased text and concept load, less reliance on visuals, longer sentences, and more literary language.

Level 4 builds reading stamina by providing more text per page, increased use of punctuation, greater variation in sentence patterns, and increasingly challenging vocabulary.

Level 5 encourages children to move from "learning to read" to "reading to learn" by providing even more text, varied writing styles, and less familiar topics.

Whichever book is right for your reader, Blastoff! Readers are the perfect books to build confidence and encourage a love of reading that will last a lifetime!

This edition first published in 2019 by Bellwether Media, Inc.

Library of Congress Cataloging-in-Publication Data

Names: Perish, Patrick, author.
Title: Roadrunners / by Patrick Perish.
Description: Minneapolis, MN : Bellwether Media, Inc., 2019. | Series: Blastoff! Readers. Animals of the Desert | Audience: Age 5-8. | Audience: K to Grade 3. | Includes bibliographical references and index.
Identifiers: LCCN 2018030998 (print) | LCCN 2018036932 (ebook) | ISBN 9781618916341 (ebook) | ISBN 9781626179233 (hardcover : alk. paper)
Subjects: LCSH: Roadrunner--Juvenile literature. | Desert animals--Juvenile literature.
Classification: LCC QL696.C83 (ebook) | LCC QL696.C83 P47 2019 (print) | DDC 598.7/4--dc23
LC record available at https://lccn.loc.gov/2018030998

Editor: Rebecca Sabelko   Designer: Josh Brink

Printed in the United States of America, North Mankato, MN

Table of Contents

Life in the Desert

Roadrunners live in the southwestern United States and northern Mexico.

This desert **biome** has wide-open lands dotted with brush.

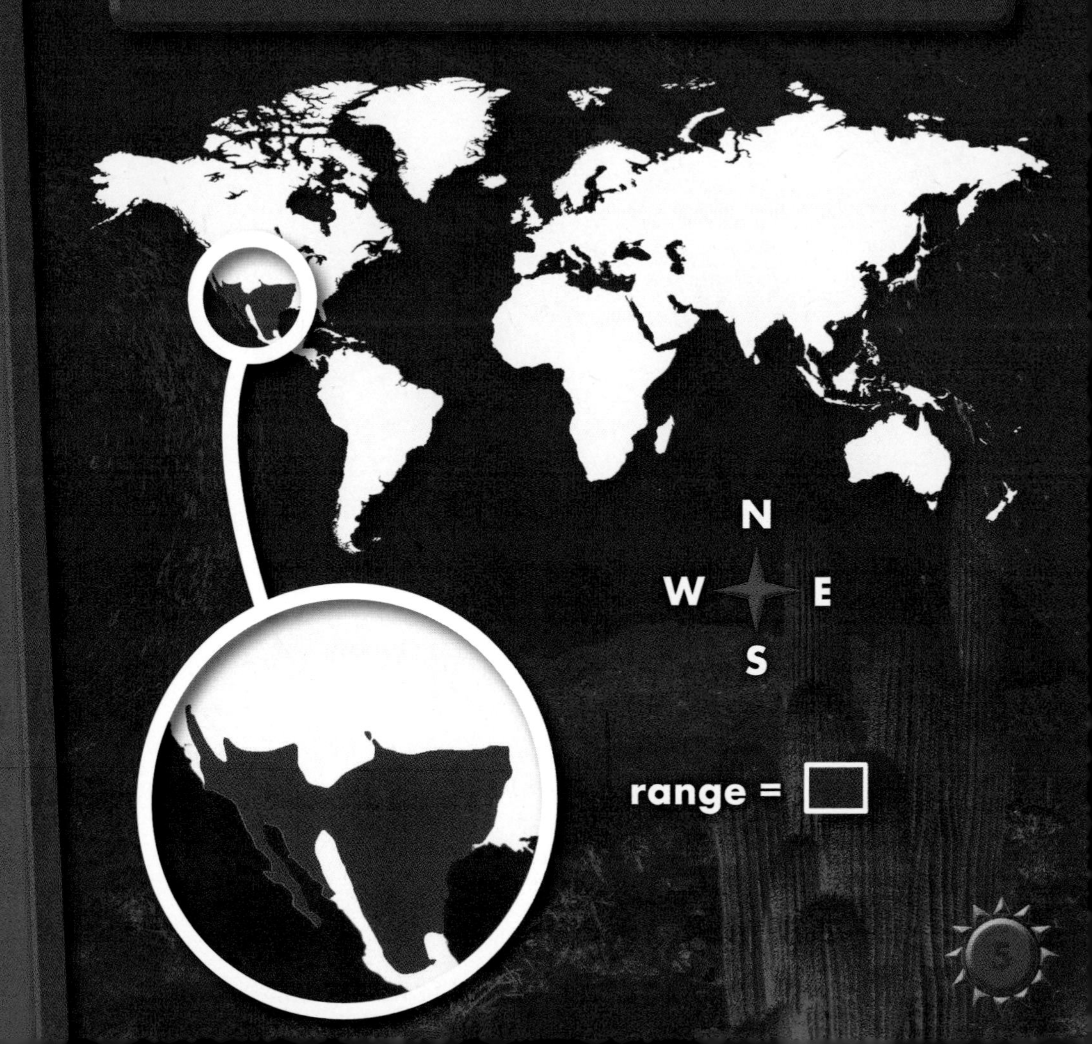

There is very little water in the desert.

Roadrunners have **adapted** to the lack of water in different ways.

Roadrunners get most of their water from food.

Their bodies pull as much water as possible from their food before they poop.

Special Adaptations

Most animals get rid of salt when they pee. But roadrunners let out salt through holes near their eyes.

This helps their bodies keep more water!

Survival Skills

Roadrunners need to be fast to catch **prey** in the open desert.

Strong legs and long tails help them run. These birds can move up to 18 miles (29 kilometers) per hour!

Deserts have cold nights. Roadrunners like to warm up in the morning sun.

Dark patches under their feathers take in heat. Soon they are ready to run!

Desert afternoons get hot. Roadrunners rest during this time to keep cool.

They find shade in
shrubs or grasses.

Birds on the Hunt

Roadrunners are excellent **predators**. They hunt birds, **rodents**, and lizards.

They also eat **insects** and fruit.

Greater Roadrunner Diet

tiger rattlesnakes

white-lined grasshoppers

lesser earless lizards

Roadrunners catch prey by running and jumping. They use their strong beaks to lift and slam prey into the ground.

They are fearless desert birds!

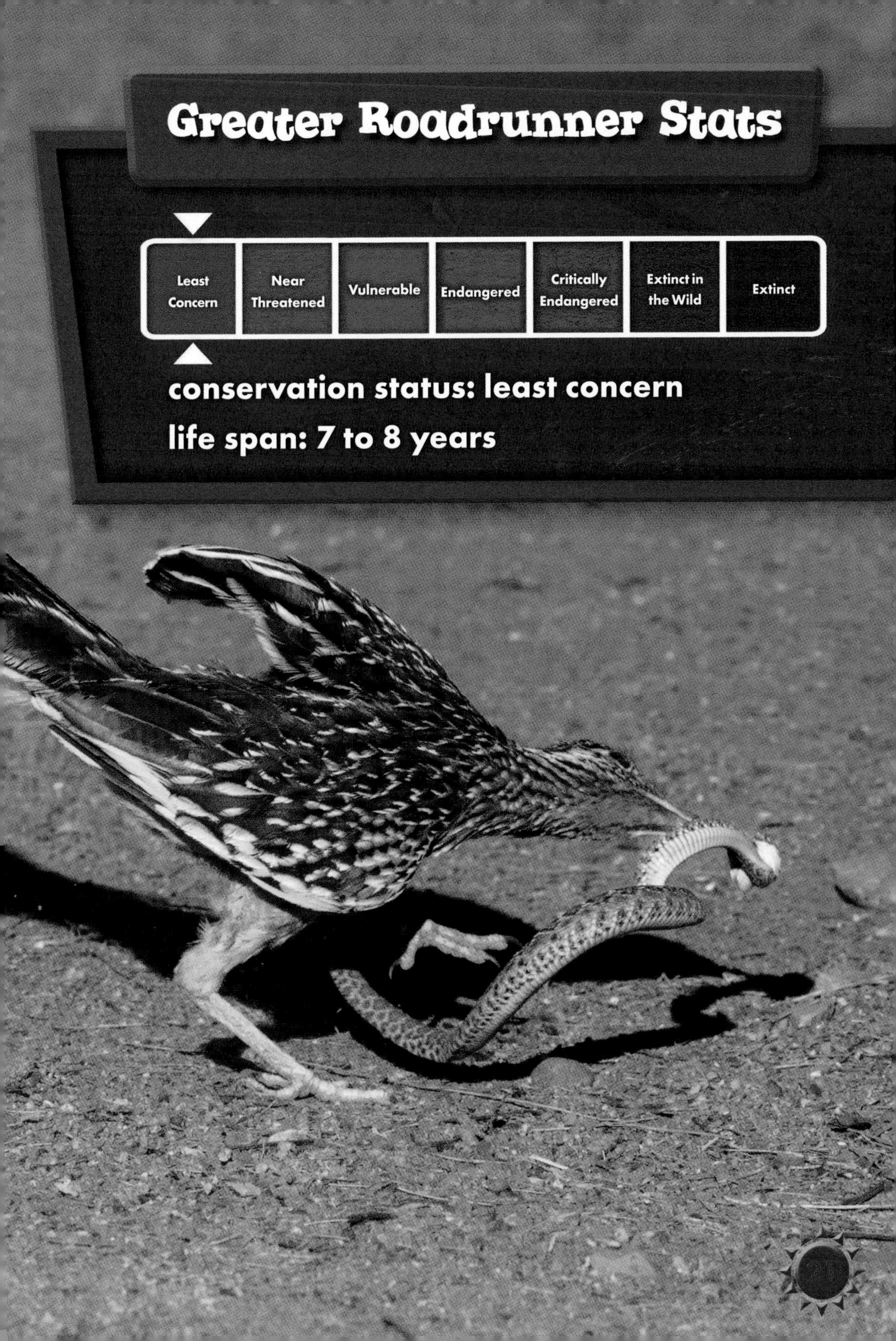

Greater Roadrunner Stats

conservation status: least concern

life span: 7 to 8 years

Glossary

adapted—changed over a long period of time

biome—a large area with certain plants, animals, and weather

insects—small animals with six legs and hard outer bodies; an insect's body is divided into three parts.

predators—animals that hunt other animals for food

prey—animals that are hunted by other animals for food

rodents—small animals that gnaw on their food; mice, rats, and squirrels are all rodents.

To Learn More

AT THE LIBRARY

Leighton, Christina. *Roadrunners.* Minneapolis, Minn.: Bellwether Media, 2017.

MacGregor, Eloise. *Roadrunner.* New York, N.Y.: Bearport Publishing, 2015.

Murray, Laura K. *In the Deserts.* Mankato, Minn.: Creative Education, 2019.

ON THE WEB

FACTSURFER

Factsurfer.com gives you a safe, fun way to find more information.

1. Go to www.factsurfer.com.

2. Enter "roadrunners" into the search box.

3. Click the "Surf" button and select your book cover to see a list of related web sites

With factsurfer.com, finding more information is just a click away.

Index

The images in this book are reproduced through the courtesy of: lalcreative, front cover; Jon Manjeot, pp. 2-3; Tim Zurowski, pp. 4, 9; SweetyMommy, p. 6; through-my-lens, p. 7; Dee Carpenter Photography, p. 8; Theron Stripling III, p. 9 (inset); Birds and Dragons, p. 10; NaturesDisplay, p. 11; Lisay, p. 12; Elizabeth W. Kearley/ Getty Images, p. 13; Dennis W Donohue, p. 14; Rick & Nora Bowers/ Alamy, pp. 15, 21; Jason Meyer/ Alamy, p. 16; Chris Howes/ Alamy, p. 17; John Cancalosi/ Alamy, p. 18; Ali Iyoob Photography, p. 19 (top left); Armbrust/ Wikipedia, p. 19 (top right); makasana, p. 19 (bottom); shootnikonrawstock/ Alamy, p. 20; Steve Bower, p. 22.